A Play

Bend, Stretch and Leap

Story by Julie Haydon

People in the Play

Reader

Tommy

Jackson

Robert

Jessica
(mime only)

Mum

Ballet Teacher

Greg Stanley

Reader
At school one day,
Tommy and his friends Jackson
and Robert were playing basketball.

Tommy *(to Jackson and Robert)*
There are lots of things
that I like to do.
I like to read,
and watch my favourite TV shows.
And I like to play basketball, too.
Look how high I can leap!
But best of all, I like to do ballet.

Reader
Every Saturday morning,
Tommy walked to the ballet school
with his sister, Jessica, and his mum.

Ballet Teacher
Stand where you can all see me.
When the music starts,
we will bend and stretch and leap.

Reader

One Saturday morning,
after ballet class,
Tommy walked to the shops
with Jessica and Mum.
He met Jackson and Robert
from school.

Jackson

Hi, Tommy.
We have been playing football.
Have you been doing ballet again?

Robert

Tommy likes ballet.

Jackson

Ballet is for girls.
Football and basketball are for boys.

Tommy

But boys do ballet, too!

I like football and basketball **and** ballet.

Reader
All that week, Tommy thought about what Jackson had said.
The next Saturday …

Tommy
Mum, I have decided I don't want to go to ballet class today.

Mum
Are you feeling sick?

Tommy
No. I just don't want to go.

Mum
Well, you will have to stay home with Gran.
I am going to take Jessica to ballet school now.

Tommy *(sadly)*
I wish I was bending
and stretching and leaping
in time to the music
at ballet school.

Reader
When Tommy arrived at school
on Monday,
Robert and Jackson rushed up to him.

Robert
We are going to have a visitor today.
He's going to meet us in the hall.

Jackson
Hey! It's Greg Stanley!

Robert
The basketball player!
He's the greatest!

Greg Stanley
Hello, boys and girls.
I'm here to talk to you
about keeping fit.
Playing sport is a good way to keep fit.
Let's do some quick warm-up exercises,
and then we'll have a game of basketball.

Reader

Everyone in the class
had a turn at playing basketball.
But no one was fitter than Tommy.
He could run faster than anyone else,
and jump higher to score a goal.

Greg Stanley

You are a very good basketball player!
I can see you are very fit.

Jackson

Tommy does ballet.
What do you think of a boy doing ballet?

Greg Stanley

I think it's a great idea.
I learned ballet when I was a boy.
It's one of the best ways to keep fit.
And it's good for your balance, too.
What do you like best
about ballet, Tommy?

Tommy

I like to bend and stretch and leap.
Ballet is great fun!